What is God Like?

Published except in the USA & Canada by

Published in the USA & Canada by

The Lutterworth Press
P. O. Box 60
Cambridge
CB1 2NT
e-mail: publishing@lutterworth.com
web site: http//www.lutterworth.com

The Liturgical Press
Collegeville
Minnesota
MN 56321

ISBN 0 7188 2973 5

ISBN 0 8146 2510 X

British Library Cataloguing in Publication Data:
A catalogue record is available from the British Library

Written by Marie-Agnès Gaudrat
Illustrated by Ulises Wensell
English Version © The Lutterworth Press 1992
This omnibus edition © The Lutterworth Press 1998
First published by The Lutterworth Press 1998
This edition first published in the USA and Canada by The Liturgical Press 1998
Originally published as
Collection Ressemblances © Bayard Presse - Centurion, 1992

Printed in China

The Love
of God

The love of God is like a hug which makes you feel warm inside.

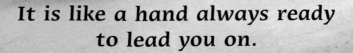

It is like a hand always ready
to lead you on.

The love of God is like a jump which carries us forward.

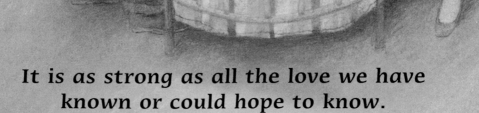

It is as strong as all the love we have
known or could hope to know.

The love of God is like a teddy bear always ready to cheer you up.

It is like a gentle tap to help you to go on.

The love of God is like a cuddle that brings you out of a sulk.

It is like the little arms which can calm
down anger.

Faith
in God

**Faith in God is like
the trust you have in your father.**

It helps you to keep your balance.

Faith in God is like a little light
shining in the dark,

When you've lost your way
it makes your heart thrill.

**Faith in God is like
the thirst you feel in summer,**

Which makes you hurry and tastes so good when you drink.

Faith in God is a bit like
the string of a kite:

It isn't the thing that we look at,
but it's what pulls us forward.

The Presence
of God

The presence of God is like the light,

The light which brightens our days.

The presence of God is like the wind,

The wind which fills us with life.

The presence of God is like the rain,

The rain which refreshes us.

The presence of God is like a rock,

A rock on which we can always lean.

The Word
of God

**The word of God is like
a fantastic present,**

The more you open it up the more it gives.

The word of God is like this light,

The more you share it
the brighter it shines.

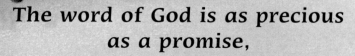

The word of God is as precious
as a promise,

A promise that is always around you,
like perfume.

The word of God is like those stories you never tire of,